Hockey GOATs

The Greatest Athletes of All Time

Published by Capstone Press, an imprint of Capstone
1710 Roe Crest Drive, North Mankato, Minnesota 56003
capstonepub.com

Library of Congress Cataloging-in-Publication Data is available on the Library of Congress website.

ISBN: 9781669062936 (hardcover)
ISBN: 9781669062998 (paperback)
ISBN: 9781669062974 (ebook PDF)

Summary: How do you pick hockey's GOATs? Wayne Gretzky and Hayley Wickenheiser get a lot of praise. But is Dominik Hašek the greatest goalie? And what about the constant Stanley Cup winners the Montreal Canadiens? It comes down to stats, history, and hunches. Read more about some of the legends of hockey and see if you agree that they're the greatest of all time.

Editorial Credits
Editor: Ericka Smith; Designer: Sarah Bennett; Media Researcher: Svetlana Zhurkin; Production Specialist: Katy LaVigne

Image Credits
Associated Press: Carlos Osorio, cover (top left), David Stluka, cover (bottom right), Lehtikuva/Antti Aimo-Koivisto, 9 (top), Peter Cosgrove, cover (bottom left), Reed Saxon, cover (top middle), The Boston Herald/Ray Lussier, 13; Getty Images: Allsport/Andy Lyons, 24, Allsport/Rick Stewart, 6, 22, Archive Photos, 17, Brian Bahr, 27, Bruce Bennett, 15, Doug Pensinger, 21, Elsa, 18, Ezra Shaw, 25, Jamie Squire, 19, 20, NHLI/Andy Devlin, 26; Shutterstock: Apostle (star background), cover and throughout, Gints Ivuskans, 5 (bottom), Iurii Osadchi, 9 (bottom), Sunward Art (star confetti), 4 and throughout; Sports Illustrated: David E. Klutho, cover (top right and bottom middle), 11, 14, 23, Erick W. Rasco, 5 (top), Richard Meek, 29

All internet sites appearing in back matter were available and accurate when this book was sent to press.

Direct Quotation
Page 26, from Jan. 16, 2019, *NBC Sports* article, "Wayne Gretzky Compares Hayley Wickenheiser to NHL Legend," nbcsports.com

All records and statistics in this book are current through 2022.

Printed and bound in China. 6667

Table of Contents

Words in **bold** appear in the glossary.

A Game of Speed and Skill

Some people call hockey the fastest game in the world. The best in the sport can skate faster than 20 miles (32 kilometers) per hour. And some players can fire slap shots at 100 mph (160 kmph).

But hockey is about more than speed. It also demands skill. Centers can put a pass on the blade of an open teammate across the ice. **Wingers** can make between-the-legs shots. Players on defense poke the puck away from forwards. And goalies use lightning reflexes to make saves.

Hockey's best players show skill and speed on the ice. That's why we remember them as the greatest of all time.

In 2022, Sarah Nurse helped Canada win the biggest prize in women's hockey—Olympic gold. Nurse set a new scoring record for modern Olympic hockey—women's and men's—with 18 points (5 goals, 13 assists) in one tournament. That was only her fourth year with the national team. If she keeps scoring, will she be one of the GOATs?

In his first nine seasons in the NHL, Connor McDavid (right) led the league in total points (goals and assists) five times. He won the Hart Trophy as league MVP three times. But his team has not won the Stanley Cup. Will lifting the cup seal McDavid's place as one of the GOATs?

Goalies: The Best Between the Pipes

Dominik Hašek

Like many National Hockey League (NHL) goalies, Dominik Hašek was tall and athletic. What set him apart from others was his flexibility. He could move in the **crease** like no one else.

Hašek (right) is the only NHL goalie to win the Hart Trophy as MVP twice.

Hašek's greatest performance happened during the 1998 Winter Olympics. Many predicted Canada would win gold. Their team was full of NHL stars. But Hašek's team, the Czech Republic, beat Canada in the semifinals. In the final shootout, Hašek stopped all five Canadian shooters. Then, he shut out Russia in the gold-medal game.

High-Performing Goalies

Hašek is at the top in two important goalie statistics—save percentage and goals against average.

Career Save Percentage

Player	Years Played	Save Percentage
Dominik Hašek	1990–2008	.9223
Johnny Bower	1953–1970	.9219
Ken Dryden	1970–1979	.9215

Career Goals Against Average

Player	Years Played	Goals Against Average
Dominik Hašek	1990–2008	2.202
Ken Dryden	1970–1979	2.238
Martin Brodeur	1991–2015	2.242

Noora Räty

The one team to challenge Canada and the United States' **dominance** in women's hockey is Finland. The biggest strength of the Finnish team has been its goalie Noora Räty.

When Räty was 18 years old, she led the Finns in a shutout win over the United States at the 2008 International Ice Hockey Federation (IIHF) Women's World Championship. She was named MVP of the tournament.

One of Räty's greatest performances was in the semifinals of the 2019 IIHF Women's World Championship. She made 43 saves to help the Finns beat Canada, 4–2.

In the final game against the United States, Räty made 50 saves. She held the Americans to a single goal in **regulation time**. After a Finnish goal in overtime was not allowed, the game went to a shootout. The United States ended up winning, but the game was a huge event across Finland.

Räty making a save against Canada during the 2019 IIHF Women's World Championship

Canada's Goalies Dominate

Dominant teams have dominant goalies. For a decade, Shannon Szabados was the dominant goalie for Team Canada. In her first Olympics, the 2010 Vancouver Games, she shut out the Americans in the gold-medal game. She won gold again in 2014.

Defense: Holding the Blue Line

Nicklas Lidström & Angela Ruggiero

When Nicklas Lidström joined the Detroit Red Wings in 1991, there were not many Europeans in the NHL. Lidström was the first European to win the Norris Trophy as the league's best defenseman. When the Red Wings won the Stanley Cup in 2008, Lidström became the first European captain of a championship team.

Angela Ruggiero also had many firsts. She played in more games for Team USA than any other hockey player. And she was the first player from California inducted into the Hockey Hall of Fame.

Players on defense need to be smart. They must **anticipate** what other players will do. Both Ruggiero and Lidström were smart defensive players. They were smart off the ice too. Lidström helped write a research paper about hockey. Ruggiero started a global sports **management** company and was an advisor for the International Olympic Committee.

Nicklas Lidström

Angela Ruggiero

Triple-Title Winners

Lidström and Ruggiero have both won three prestigious championships in men's and women's hockey.

Nicklas Lidström

Award	Team	Year(s)
Stanley Cup	Detroit Red Wings	1997, 1998, 2002, 2008
Olympic Gold Medal	Team Sweden	2006
IIHF World Championship	Team Sweden	1991

Angela Ruggiero

Award	Team	Year(s)
NCAA Hockey Championship	Harvard University	1999
Olympic Gold Medal	Team USA	1998
IIHF World Championship	Team USA	2005, 2008, 2009, 2011

Bobby Orr

Sometimes a GOAT transforms the way a sport is played. This was the case with Bobby Orr.

The defense's job is just to keep the other team from scoring. Orr did that—and more. When Orr got the puck, he made things happen. With speed and impressive stickhandling, Orr could carry the puck from end to end. He would find open teammates to set up a goal. Sometimes he would fire a shot himself.

Orr smashed scoring records for defensive players. He became the first defenseman to tally 100 points in a season. And he was the first NHL player in any position to have 100 assists in a season.

Award-Winning Defense

Orr has won the Norris Trophy more than any other player.

Player	Team	Number of Norris Trophy Wins
Bobby Orr	Boston Bruins	8
Nicklas Lidström	Detroit Red Wings	7
Doug Harvey	Montreal Canadiens	7

One of the most famous photos in sports history shows Orr flying through the air after scoring a goal. Orr had just scored the winning goal in the 1970 Stanley Cup Finals.

Wingers: Leading the Attack

Cammi Granato

The first job of a winger is to score goals. Nobody has scored more points for the U.S. women's hockey team than Cammi Granato. In 205 games, she scored 186 goals. She also made 157 assists, giving her 343 total points.

Granato (front) playing for the United States in the 2002 Olympics

Granato played for Team USA at the first IIHF Women's World Championship in 1990. She also scored the first Olympic goal for the team at the 1998 Nagano Games. The Americans ended up winning gold.

After retiring as a player, Granato became one of the first women to have a management role with an NHL team. She was a **scout** for the Kraken. Soon after, she became the assistant **general manager** for the Canucks.

Granato (right) was one of the first two women inducted into the IIHF Hall of Fame. The other was Angela James (left). Playing center and defense, James was the top scorer for Canada in the first international women's tournaments in the 1990s.

Gordie Howe

There is one name at the top of the list of greatest NHL wingers—Gordie Howe. Howe was a legend. He was known simply as "Mr. Hockey."

Howe used his strength and toughness to win battles for the puck. He could score. And he could set up teammates. He was the first NHL player to lead the league in scoring four straight seasons. He was also one of the league's top five scorers for 20 straight seasons.

Howe was known for his **durability** too. He played 25 seasons for the Red Wings. Then he played six seasons in the World Hockey Association. In 1979, he played one more season in the NHL. He was 52 years old when he played his last game.

When Howe retired, he held the records for most goals, assists, and total points.

Howe (front) playing for the Red Wings in a 1965 game against the New York Rangers

Centers: Covering the Ice

Mark Messier & Sidney Crosby

Centers cover more ice than any other player. They are also team leaders. This was the case with two of the greatest centers in NHL history—Mark Messier and Sidney Crosby.

Messier won the Stanley Cup five times with the Edmonton Oilers, so the New York Rangers signed him hoping that he would lead them to their first championship.

Messier is the only person to captain two Stanley Cup-winning teams—the Oilers in 1990 and the Rangers in 1994.

During the 1994 playoffs, the Rangers were close to **elimination**. Messier **guaranteed** the team's win. The Rangers won that series and later the Stanley Cup.

Crosby has led Pittsburgh to three Stanley Cup championships. But his biggest win came at the 2010 Winter Olympics. Crosby scored the overtime goal for Canada in the final game against the United States. Canadians celebrate Crosby's "golden goal" as one of the greatest in hockey history.

In 2010, Crosby (in white) won the Mark Messier NHL Leadership Award, which is presented to the player who is a leader on and off the ice.

Brianna Decker & Marie-Philip Poulin

The two best teams in women's hockey are the United States and Canada. Two of the best players in women's hockey were the top centers for Team USA and Team Canada.

Brianna Decker has been winning since college. At the University of Wisconsin, she won a national championship. She also led Team USA to Olympic gold in 2018. They also won six titles at the IIHF Women's World Championship.

Decker competed in the passing event at the 2019 NHL All-Star Skills Competition. She did better than all the NHL players who competed.

Poulin (center) is the only player in hockey history—women's or men's—to score the winning goal in three Olympic finals.

Marie-Philip Poulin is known as "Captain Clutch." She scores when the pressure is on. She scored the winning goals for Canada in gold-medal games at the Olympics in 2010, 2014, and 2022.

The Best Rivalry in Hockey

Since the first world championship in women's hockey in 1990, Team USA and Team Canada have won every international title in women's hockey.

	Olympic Gold Medals	IIHF Women's World Championship Wins
Canada	5	13
United States	2	10

Mario Lemieux

The greatest players make some of the best moments happen. On December 27, 2000, Mario Lemieux achieved one of those moments when he stepped on the ice to play for the Pittsburgh Penguins. He had retired more than three years earlier. But that night, he was back on the ice.

Thirty-three seconds into the game, Lemieux assisted on a goal by Jaromir Jagr. In the second period, Lemieux scored a goal. Later, he assisted on another. The Penguins won 5–0. "Super Mario" was back!

Coming Back Again and Again

Lemieux played 17 seasons in the NHL. But he never played a full season of 82 games. Lemieux battled serious health problems throughout his career. He had such terrible back pain that he needed someone else to tighten his skates. He missed the entire 1994–95 season due to cancer treatment. When he came back the following season, he led the NHL in scoring and won the Hart Trophy as MVP.

Before his retirement, Lemieux had led the league in scoring six times. He had been named league MVP three times. He had also captained the Penguins to two Stanley Cup titles. That night, Lemieux reminded hockey fans he was one of the GOATs.

Only two players in NHL history have finished a season with more than 160 total points—Lemieux (right) and Wayne Gretzky.

Legends

Wayne Gretzky

Just one player in NHL history has his number retired across the league—Wayne Gretzky. No one in the NHL will wear the number 99 again.

Gretzky has the most goals in NHL history. He also holds the record for most goals in a season—92 during the 1981–82 season. But he was even better as a passer. Gretzky and only two other players have more than 100 assists in a season. Bobby Orr and Mario Lemieux did it just once. Gretzky had more than 100 assists in 11 seasons!

Gretzky is the only NHL player to get more than 200 points in a season. He did it four times.

Gretzky holds some amazing records that no NHL player will beat. Perhaps the most amazing is his total points record. If you took away all 894 goals he scored in his career, his 1,963 assists would still give him the most total points of any player in hockey history.

Top Career NHL Scorers

Player	Number of Seasons	Goals	Assists	Total Points
Wayne Gretzky	20	894	1963	2857
Jaromir Jagr	24	766	1155	1921
Mark Messier	25	694	1193	1887
Gordie Howe	26	801	1049	1850

Hayley Wickenheiser

When Hayley Wickenheiser retired from hockey, Wayne Gretzky was there to pay tribute to her. "You played with heart, desire, **finesse**, speed, skill," said Gretzky.

Wickenheiser is the highest scorer in history for the Canadian women's hockey team. In 276 international games, she scored 168 goals. She had 211 assists too.

Wickenheiser (right) competed in five Winter Olympics as a hockey player. She was such a great athlete that she also competed in the 2000 Summer Olympics for the Canadian national softball team.

Wickenheiser was an extraordinary player at a time when women's hockey was just beginning to gain attention. When she started, Wickenheiser had to play on boys' teams because there were no girls' teams. By the time she retired, there were teams and leagues for girls across North America.

GOAT Players on the GOAT Team

The Montreal Canadiens have won the Stanley Cup more than any other team. Several times the Canadiens had a dominant group of players who won multiple titles in a row.

In the 1960s, the Canadiens won the Stanley Cup four times in five seasons.

In the 1970s, with goalie Ken Dryden, the Canadiens won the Stanley Cup six times, including four years in a row.

But the greatest Canadiens **dynasty** was in the 1950s. The Canadiens won the Stanley Cup for five straight seasons. No other NHL team has done that. On that Canadiens team were four players who rank among the greatest in their positions—center Jean Béliveau, left wing Maurice Richard, defenseman Doug Harvey, and goalie Jacques Plante.

No other NHL team has been stacked with so many GOATs.

Harvey (left) behind the net during the 1957 Stanley Cup Finals against the Boston Bruins

Glossary

anticipate (an-TIS-uh-payt)—to expect something to happen

crease (KREES)—the area directly in front of the goal in hockey; it's often painted blue

dominance (DOM-uh-nuhns)—in sports, winning much more than anyone else

durability (duhr-uh-BIL-ih-tee)—the ability to last over time

dynasty (DYE-nuh-stee)—a team that wins multiple championships over a period of several years

elimination (i-li-muh-NAY-shuhn)—removed from competition by losing

finesse (fih-NESS)—expert skill in something

general manager (JEN-ur-uhl MAN-uh-jur)—for a professional sports team, the person who signs players and makes trades

guarantee (gar-uhn-TEE)—to make sure that something will happen

management (MAN-ij-muhnt)—in sports, running the business of teams or leagues

regulation time (reg-yuh-LEY-shuhn TYM)—the set duration for an ordinary game; in hockey, three periods

scout (SKOUT)—in sports, a person who judges the skills of young players and recommends whether a professional team should sign them

winger (WING-uhr)—a person who plays on the left and right sides of the rink

Read More

Bullaro, Angie. *Breaking the Ice: The True Story of the First Woman to Play in the National Hockey League.* New York: Simon & Schuster, 2020.

Flynn, Brendan. *Extreme Sports GOATs: The Greatest Athletes of All Time.* North Mankato, MN: Capstone, 2024.

Walker, Tracy Sue. *Wayne Gretzky: The Great One.* Minneapolis: Lerner, 2023.

Internet Sites

International Ice Hockey Federation
iihf.com

National Hockey League
nhl.com

International Olympic Committee: Hockey
olympics.com/en/sports/hockey

Index

photo by Marta Berglund

About the Author

Bruce Berglund played baseball, hockey, and football as a kid. When he got older, he was a coach and referee. Bruce taught college history for many years. He wrote a history book for adults on world hockey. He is now writing a book about the history of referees and umpires.